TO THE TEACHER

The THEORY DRILL GAMES are designed to teach Musical Rudiments in an interesting and attractive manner, while saving valuable time at the lesson period. All the work is done at home and the teacher can quickly evaluate the pupils' efforts as the work sheets are handed in for examination.

It has long been recognized that the quickest and best way to master NOTATION, TIME, RHYTHM and all other elements of music, is by means of WRITING EXERCISES. Unfortunately, the theoretical side of music study is usually the least attractive, from the student's viewpoint, and the difficulty has been that of capturing the interest and attention of young pupils to the point where they are willing to do the work by themselves at home.

To help overcome this hazard, the work has been presented here in the form of MUSICAL GAMES or PUZZLES. It offers a DO-IT-YOURSELF plan in that each step is described pictorially in the form of ANIMATED DRAWINGS or COMIC STRIPS, so popular with the average child. This obviates the necessity for lengthy explanations during the lesson period and, at the same time, injects a bit of humor into what otherwise might be considered a "dry" subject.

The Games are presented in LOOSE LEAF form and it is most important that the pupil be given ONE LEAF AT A TIME, not the whole book at once. In this way, the drawings and musical puzzles contained in future games will retain their newness and come as a surprise to the pupil, who then looks forward with anticipation to each successive lesson. For identification, the pupil's name should be written on the front of the folder in the space provided. The set of papers is then kept in the studio and assigned *one game at a time* at the desired intervals.

It will be seen, at a glance, that the THEORY DRILL GAMES are equally adaptable to private or class instruction.

John Thompson

Copyright, MCMLVII, by the Willis Music Co.
International Copyright Secured
Printed in U. S. A.

CONTENTS OF BOOK THREE

BOOK THREE

THEORY DRILL GAME, No. 1

Leger Lines above the Bass

Pupil's Name_____   Grade (or Star) _____

Leger Lines are little lines added to the staff upon which to write more notes.

1. Trace and copy these new notes, then write their letter-names. Remember, all lines *above* Middle C are Treble lines, borrowed and brought down into the Bass.

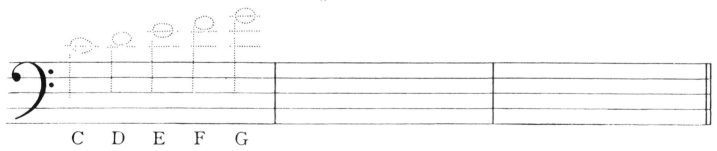

C   D   E   F   G

2. Write the letter-names of these notes.

Letter-names:

Date_____

3. Transpose these notes one octave lower in the Bass.

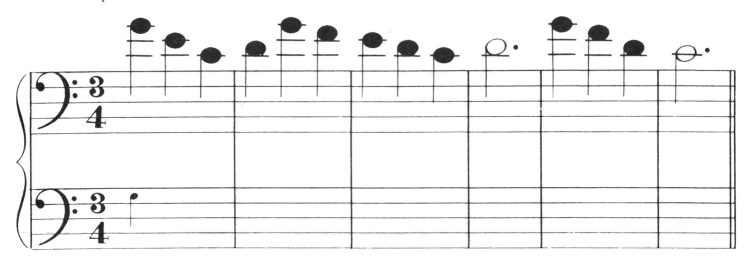

4. Transpose these notes one octave higher in the Bass.

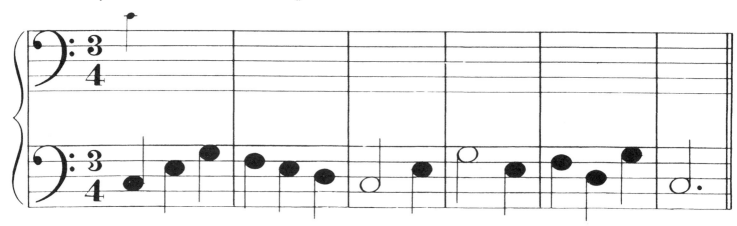

5. First write the counts, then the letter-names of these notes.

Counts:

Letter-
names:

BOOK THREE

THEORY DRILL GAME, No. 2

Leger Lines below the Treble

Pupil's Name_____   Grade (or Star) _____

Leger Lines below Middle C are borrowed lines from the Bass.

1. Trace and copy these new notes, then write their letter-names. Remember, all lines *below* Middle C are Bass lines, borrowed and brought up into the Treble.

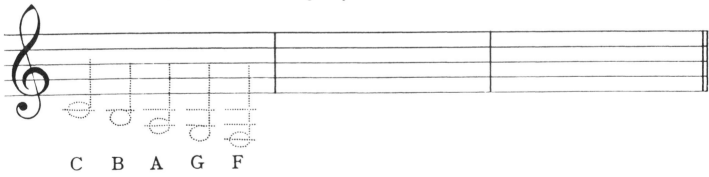

C   B   A   G   F

2. First write the counts, then the letter-names of these notes.

Counts:

Letter-names:

Date_____

3. Transpose these notes one octave higher in the Treble.

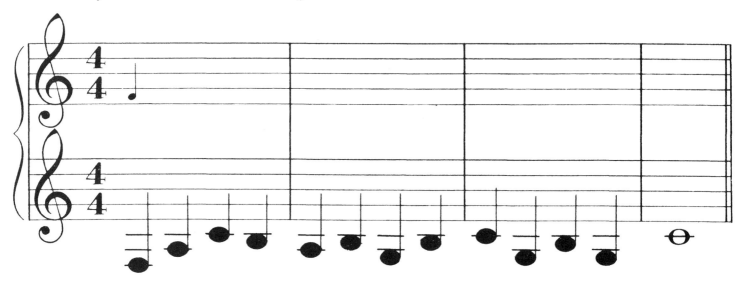

4. Transpose these notes one octave lower in the Treble.

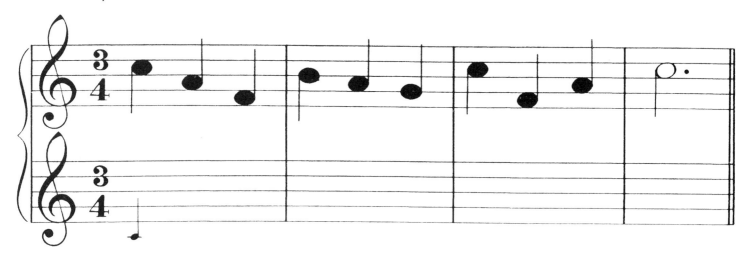

5. First write the counts, then the letter-names of these notes.

Counts:

Letter-
names:

BOOK THREE
THEORY DRILL GAME, No.
The Flying Aces

Pupil's Name_____   Grade (or Star) _____

| The Leger Lines *above* the Treble and *below* the Bass are easy to remember if you think of the Two Flying ACES. | This ACE is an altitude flyer. He flies high above the Treble. His Leger Lines spell his name, A C E. | This ACE is a hedge-hopper. He flies low below the Bass. His Leger Lines also spell A C E. |

1. Trace these notes of the High-Flying Ace. Then copy them 3 times and write their letter-names.

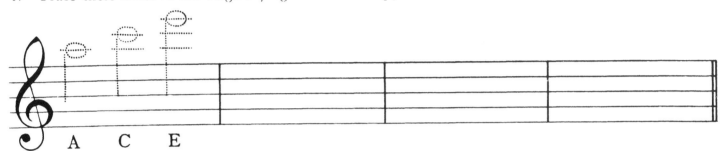

2. Trace these notes of the Low-Flying Ace. Then copy them 3 times and write their letter-names.

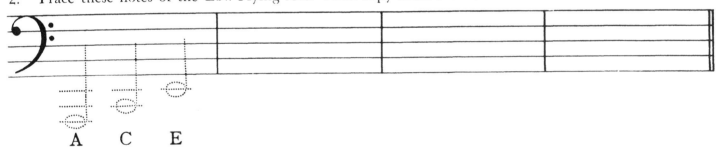

3. Write the letter-names of these notes.

Letter-names:

4. Write the letter-names of these notes.

Letter-names:

Date_____

Mission Accomplished

5. Spell the missing words.

The Commanding Officer _____ information about the enemy who was encamped at the _____ of a cliff which made _____ barrier. He explained the mission to two of his best flyers, each an _____ One was to fly low at a _____ distance in sight of the enemy. This would distract his attention while the other _____ took pictures from high above. Getting _____ focus on his camera, the high-flying _____ made pictures till the light _____ , when he signaled his partner to return. On the way _____ the low-flying _____ had motor trouble and looked for _____ place to land. He felt sure he was going to meet the enemy _____ to _____ But suddenly his motor recovered and both flyers returned _____ and sound. Their Superior Officer commended them for a fine _____ well done.

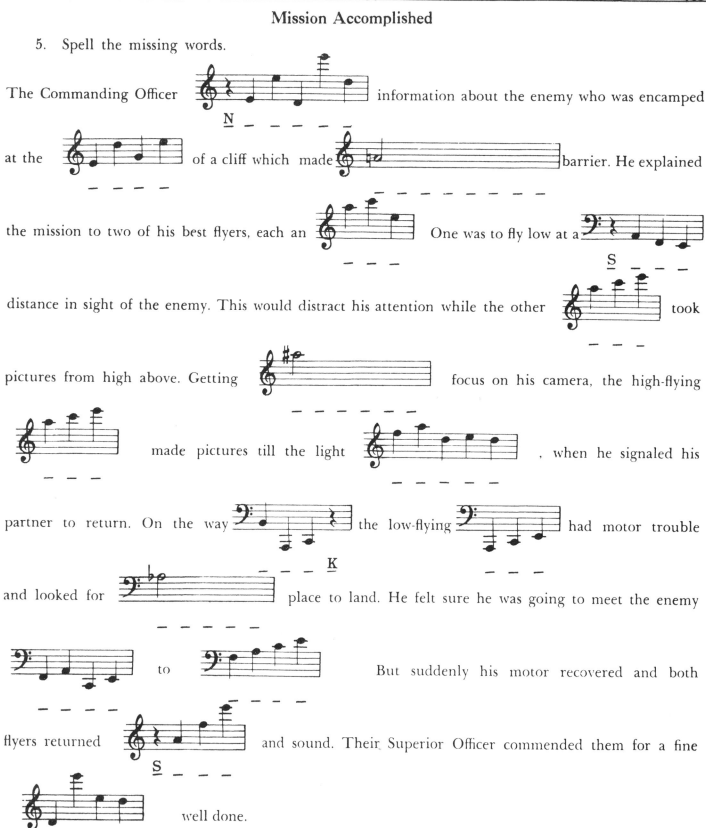

BOOK THREE

THEORY DRILL GAME, No. 4
Leger Spaces

Pupil's Name_____   Grade (or Star) _____

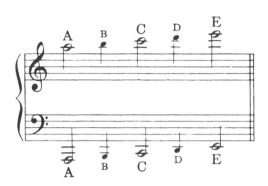

1. Write the letter-names of these notes.

Letter-names:

2.

Letter-names:

3. Write the counts and mark the accents in the following.
   Accents:

Counts:

Date_____

4. Transpose the following one octave higher in the Treble.

5. Transpose the following one octave lower in the Bass.

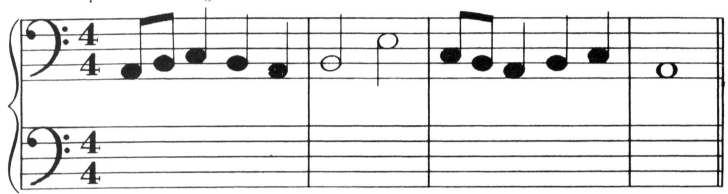

6. Write the letter-names of the following.

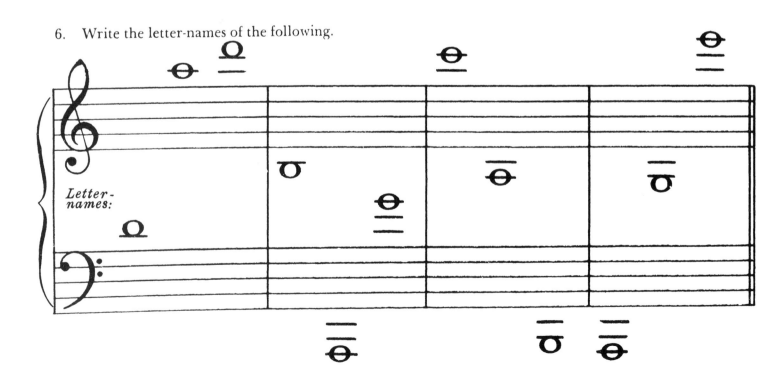

Letter-
names:

BOOK THREE
THEORY DRILL GAME, No. 5

Pupil's Name_____   Grade (or Star) _____

THREE THINGS TO DO IN THIS GAME: FIRST, DRAW THE BAR LINES; NEXT, WRITE THE COUNTS; THEN, MARK THE ACCENTS.

Date_____

THIS IS A REVIEW OF LEGER LINES AND SPACES. SEE HOW MANY YOU CAN DO CORRECTLY. REMEMBER THE FLYING ACES AND THE BORROWED LINES.

4. Spell these words on Leger Lines and Spaces above the Treble.

A C E   D A D   C A B   D E E D

Spell these words on Leger Lines and Spaces below the Treble.

C A B   B A G   F A D   G A G

5. Spell these words on Leger Lines and Spaces above the Bass.

B E D   D E E D   F E D   B E G G E D

Spell these words on Leger Lines and Spaces below the Bass.

A C E   C A D   F A C E   D E A F

BOOK THREE

THEORY DRILL GAME, No. 6

Half Steps

Pupil's Name_____   Grade (or Star)_____

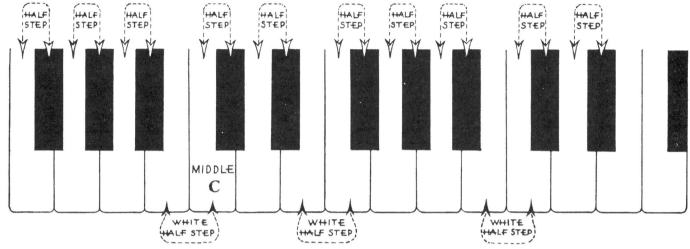

A HALF STEP is the distance between any key and THE NEXT NEAREST KEY.

Most HALF STEPS lie between a white key and a black key.

There are, however, two WHITE HALF STEPS — one between B and C and the other between E and F. Study them on the chart above and locate them on your piano keyboard.

Chromatic and Diatonic Half Steps

CHROMATIC HALF STEP

DIATONIC HALF STEP

When both notes of the Half Step have the SAME LETTER-NAME, the interval is called a CHROMATIC Half Step.

When the notes of a Half Step have TWO DIFFERENT NAMES, the interval is called a DIATONIC Half Step.

Date_____

12

1. Mark the kind of Half Steps shown in the following, using D for Diatonic and C for Chromatic.

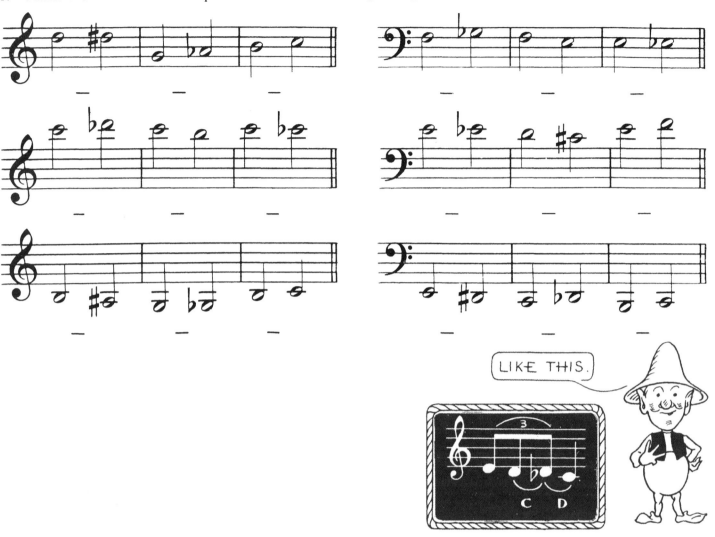

2. The Half Steps in the following are shown by curved lines.
Using the letters C and D, indicate whether they are Chromatic or Diatonic.

3. There are ten Half Steps in the following. Mark them with a curved line and indicate whether they are Chromatic or Diatonic Half Steps. Use the letters C and D.

BOOK THREE
THEORY DRILL GAME, No. 7
Whole Steps

Pupil's Name_____   Grade (or Star) _____

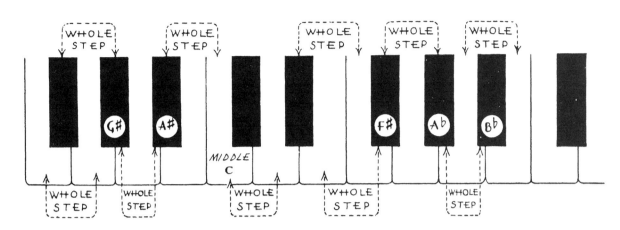

A WHOLE STEP is twice as big as a Half Step — therefore there will always be one key (either white or black) lying in between.

MARK THE WHOLE AND HALF STEPS IN THE FOLLOWING. USE **W** FOR WHOLE STEPS AND **H** FOR HALF STEPS.

1.

Date_____

2. Write a Chromatic Half Step UPWARD from each of the following.

3. Write a Chromatic Half Step DOWNWARD from each of the following.

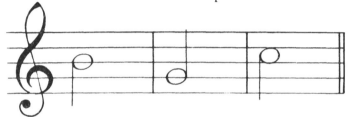 

4. Write a Diatonic Half Step UPWARD from each of the following.

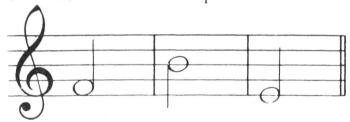 

5. Write a Diatonic Half Step DOWNWARD from each of the following.

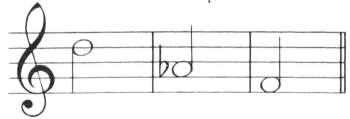 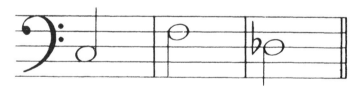

6. Write a Whole Step UPWARD from each of the following.

7. Write a Whole Step DOWNWARD from each of the following.

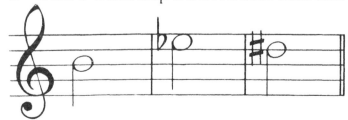 

THEORY DRILL GAME, No. 8

Pupil's Name_____ Grade (or Star) _____

TRANSPOSE THE MELODIES BELOW AS INDICATED.
1ST. – JUST WRITE THE NOTE-HEADS.
2ND. – ADD STEMS AND BEAMS, ETC.
3RD. – EXAMINE EACH NOTE TO SEE WHETHER
A SHARP, FLAT OR NATURAL SIGN IS NECESSARY.
Reference to the Chart will be a big help,
as the Keyboard is arranged in Half Steps.

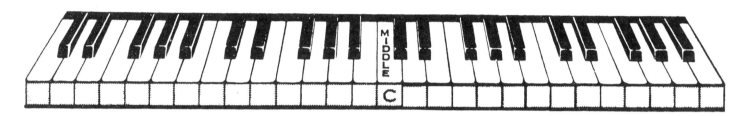

1. Transpose the Melody one Diatonic Half Step higher.

Transpose the Melody one Diatonic Half Step lower.

2. Transpose the Melody one Whole Step higher.

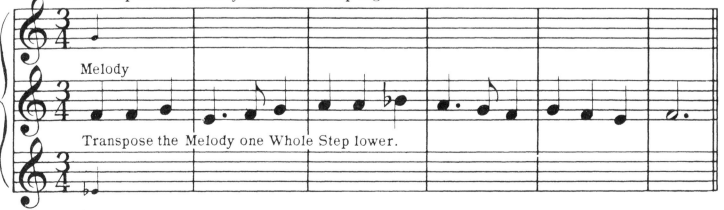

Transpose the Melody one Whole Step lower.

Date_____

4. Transpose these notes two octaves lower on the Bass staff.

5. Transpose these notes two octaves higher on the Treble staff.

BOOK THREE

THEORY DRILL GAME, No. 9
The Major Scale

Pupil's Name_____   Grade (or Star) _____

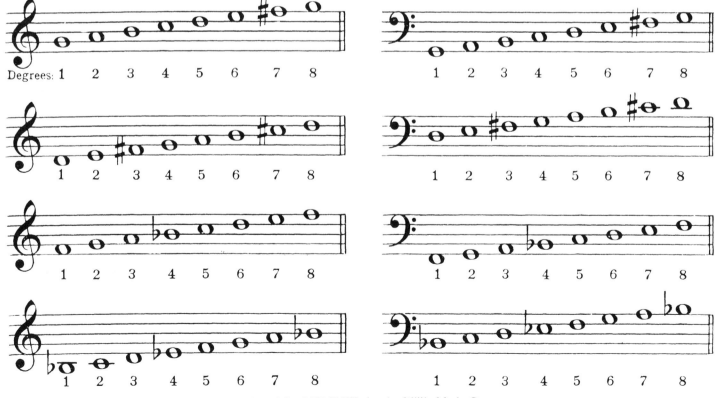

A Scale is a succession of eight tones in alphabetical order, the last tone having the same name as the first.

The notes of a Scale are numbered – one to eight. The numbers stand for the Degrees of the Scale.

In the Major Scale there must always be a Half Step between the 3rd and 4th degrees and between the 7th and 8th degrees. All others are Whole Steps.

1. Mark the Half Steps in the following Major Scales. Use a curved line as in the drawing above.

Date_____

2. Write the Major Scales as indicated below, *using Accidentals* as needed to preserve the Scale pattern — Whole Step, Whole Step, HALF STEP,
Whole Step, Whole Step, Whole Step, HALF STEP.

Mark the Half Steps with a curved line.

After each Scale is written, write its Key Signature.

THIS IS HOW THE SHARPS ARE PLACED.

Key Signatures

Sharp Scales

THEORY DRILL GAME, No. 10

Pupil's Name_____   Grade (or Star) _____

DRAW THE BAR LINES
AND MARK THE COUNTS
IN THE FOLLOWING.

1.

Counts:

Counts:

Counts:

TRANSPOSE THE FOLLOWING
ONE WHOLE STEP LOWER.
USE ACCIDENTALS.

2.

Date_____

3. Write the Major Scales as indicated below, *using Accidentals* as needed.
After each Scale is written, write its Key Signature.

Mark the Half Steps with a curved line.

THIS IS THE WAY
THE FLATS ARE PLACED.

Flat Scales

Key
Signatures

BOOK THREE

THEORY DRILL GAME, No. 11

Key Signatures (Sharps)

Pupil's Name_____   Grade (or Star) _____

NO SHARPS NOR FLATS. KEY OF C MAJOR.

ONLY ONE SHARP (F#) IS SHOWN. KEY-NOTE IS G (ONE HALF STEP HIGHER).

TWO SHARPS, F# AND C#. LAST SHARP IS C#. KEY-NOTE IS D, ONE HALF STEP HIGHER THAN C#.

| When no sharps nor flats appear in the Sigature, the piece is in the Key of C Major. | When one sharp (F#) appears in the Signature, the Key-note is one *half step* higher — Key of G Major. | When more than one sharp appears in the Signature, the Key-note is always one half step higher than the *last* sharp. Key of D Major. |

1. Copy this Key Signature three times. Be sure to place the sharps in correct order.

2. Write the Key name of each of these Major Signatures

Key:

Key:

Date_____

3. Theme from Mozart.

4. Transpose the Mozart Theme one Diatonic Half Step higher.

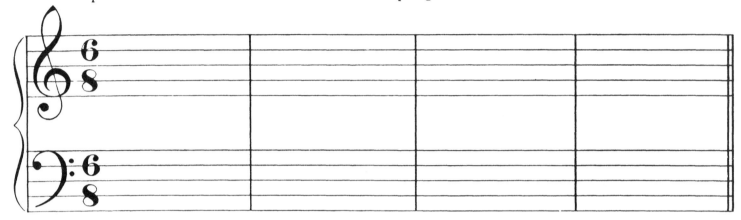

5. Transpose the Mozart Theme one Whole Step lower.

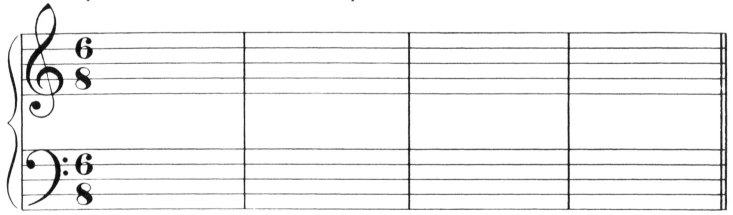

6. Now transpose what you have written above, in Ex. 5, one Whole Step still lower.

BOOK THREE

THEORY DRILL GAME, No. 12

Key Signatures (Flats)

Pupil's Name_____   Grade (or Star) _____

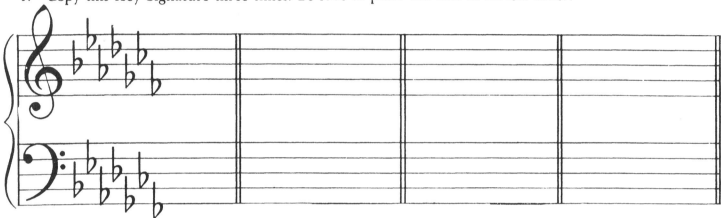

1. Copy this Key Signature three times. Be sure to place the flats in correct order.

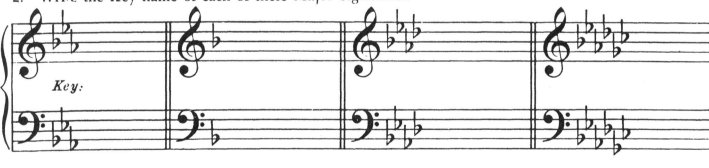

2. Write the Key name of each of these Major Signatures.

Date_____

24

3. Transpose these notes to Leger Lines *above* the Treble staff.

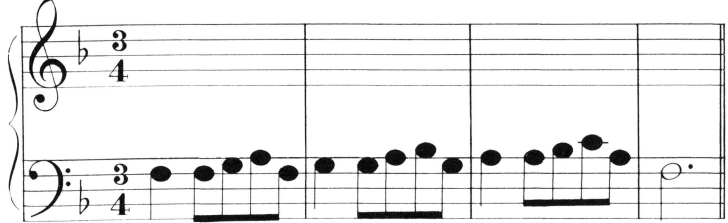

4. Transpose these notes to Leger Lines *below* the Treble staff.

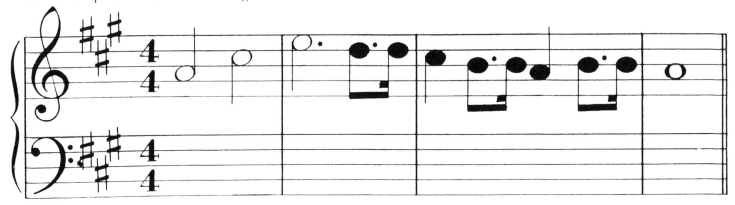

5. Transpose these notes to Leger Lines *below* the Bass staff.

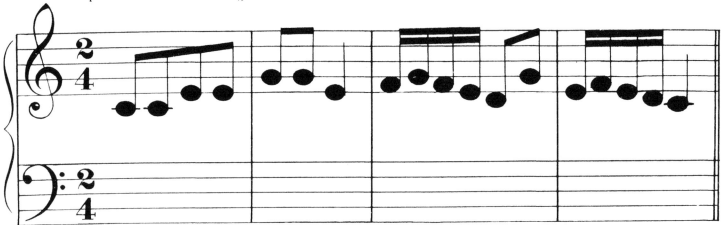

6. Transpose these notes to Leger Lines *above* the Bass staff.

BOOK THREE

THEORY DRILL GAME, No. 13

Pupil's Name_____ Grade (or Star) _____

1. Change the following into four-four by *doubling* the value of each note or rest.

2. Change the following into two-four by re-writing each note for *half* its value.

3. Change the following into three-four.

Date_____

4. Write the following Key Signatures and name the Keys.

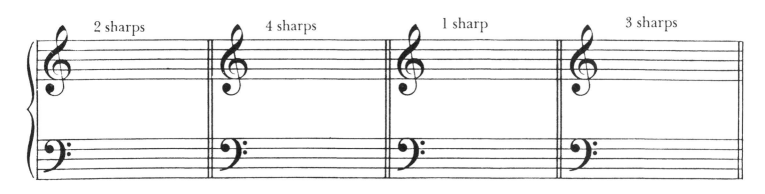

2 sharps   4 sharps   1 sharp   3 sharps

6 sharps   5 sharps   7 sharps

5. Draw the bar lines, write the counts and mark the accents in the following.

BOOK THREE

THEORY DRILL GAME, No. 14
The Chromatic Scale

Pupil's Name_____   Grade (or Star)_____

A CHROMATIC SCALE is one which progresses upward or downward by *Half Steps only*.

The Half Steps may be either Chromatic Half Steps or Diatonic Half Steps.

There are various rules for the correct 'spelling' of Chromatic Scales. For the present we shall use the easy one adopted by many composers, i.e.,

USE ONLY SHARPS WHEN THE SCALE GOES UP.
USE ONLY FLATS WHEN THE SCALE GOES DOWN.

THIS SHOWS THE ASCENDING CHROMATIC SCALE, USING SHARPS.

THIS SHOWS THE DESCENDING CHROMATIC SCALE, USING FLATS.

1. Write Chromatic Scales upward for one octave, using only sharps.

2. Write Chromatic Scales downward for one octave, using only flats.

Date_____

3. Write the following Key Signatures and name the Keys.

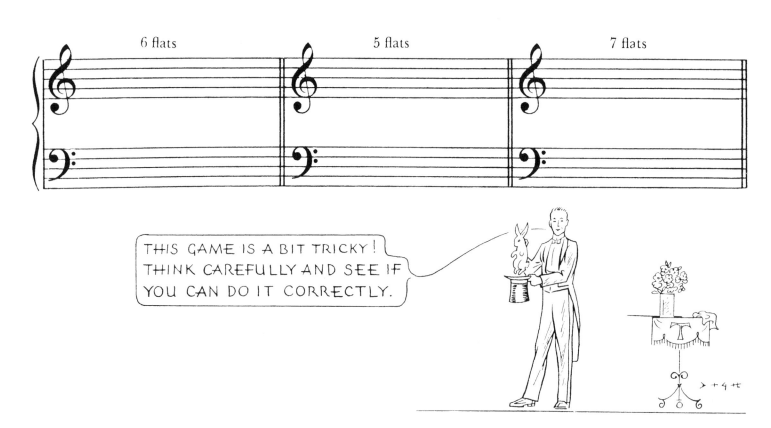

4. Join the stems with beams (single or double) so that each measure will have the correct number of counts.

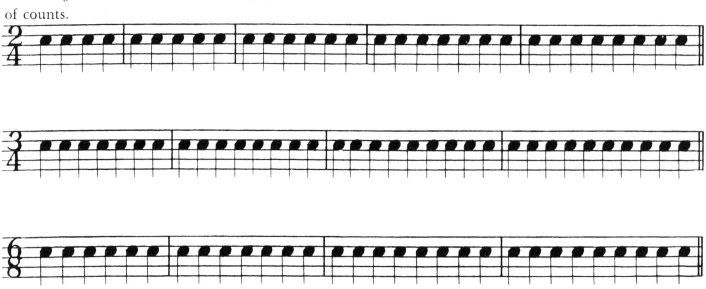

THEORY DRILL GAME, No. 15

Double Sharps and Double Flats

Pupil's Name_____   Grade (or Star) _____

1. Write the letter-names of these notes in their proper places on the keyboard.

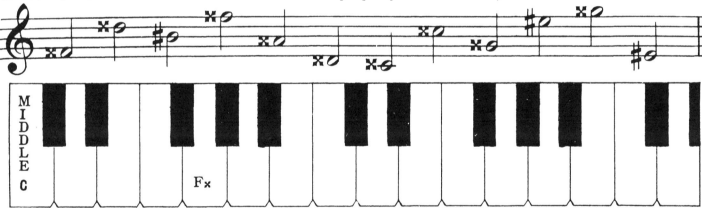

2. Write the letter-names of these notes in their proper places on the keyboard.

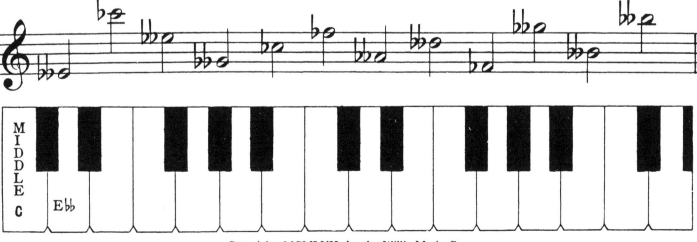

Date_____

TWO FOLLOW-UP BOOKS

Having finished Book Three of the THEORY DRILL GAMES, the pupil is now ready to proceed with John Thompson's SCALE SPELLER, a Writing Book which reviews the Major Scales and introduces Minor Scales in Natural, Melodic and Harmonic forms.

INTERVALS are also taught in this book and easy rules given, which enable the pupil to identify all Scales and Intervals BY EAR as well as BY EYE. A SCALE FINGERING CHART is given for reference at the end of the book.

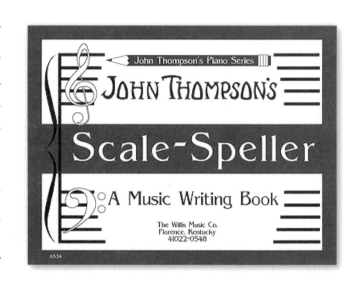

The CHORD SPELLER is also a Writing Book for Home Work. Major, minor, augmented and diminished Triads hold no terrors for the pupil who has mastered Intervals in the preceding SPELLER. Inversions, Cadence Chords, Dominant and Diminished Sevenths follow in logical order.

Again the pupil is taught to recognize all chords by SOUND as well as by SIGHT.